I0166109

James Selwin Tait

National Banks and Government Circulation

Retrospective and Prospective

James Selwin Tait

National Banks and Government Circulation
Retrospective and Prospective

ISBN/EAN: 9783337076535

Printed in Europe, USA, Canada, Australia, Japan

Cover: Foto ©Suzi / pixelio.de

More available books at **www.hansebooks.com**

NATIONAL BANKS

AND

GOVERNMENT CIRCULATION

RETROSPECTIVE AND PROSPECTIVE

BY

JAMES SELWIN TAIT, F. R. L. S.

STATISTICIAN OF

THE NORTH AMERICAN EXCHANGE CO., LIMITED.

———————•••———————

NEW YORK:

THE NORTH AMERICAN EXCHANGE CO., LIMITED.

57 Broadway, New York.

1888.

PREFACE.

The conclusions arrived at in the process of enquiry resulting in this pamphlet imply too much of a change in National Banking and Government circulation to be quoted as a mere *dictum* of the writer, unsupported by any statement of the grounds upon which his deductions are based. For that reason, and in order as far as possible to anticipate all enquiry, the writer has been careful to furnish complete data, and to weigh well the opinions already expressed by others on these subjects. He has also endeavored to reply, in advance, to such criticism as a positive opinion on any vexed question is apt to arouse. For the rest, he has only to emphasize the fact that what he counsels is reformation and not revolution, such reformation as, *inter alia*, will improve the conntry's circulation, will strengthen enormously the hold of the National Banking system upon the commerce of the country, and will bring it into harmonious relations with the Government.

The writer desires to tender his acknowledgments to the Hon. W. L. Trenholm, Comptroller of the Currency, for the courtesy with which he has from time to time complied with his requests for information on subjects within his Department.

CONTENTS.

————————

NATIONAL BANKS

AND

GOVERNMENT CIRCULATION,

RETROSPECTIVE AND PROSPECTIVE.

The trend of events in relation to the National Banks and Government currency seems to be in the following directions :—

(1.) The gradual extinction of National Banks as constituted under the Act of 1864 ; (2.) the total surrender and restriction of the currency to the Government's hands ; (3.) the reorganization of the National Banks under a new Act more in accordance with the requirements of the times ; and (4.) the withdrawal, by degrees, of Government inspection from these banks.

A reference to the recent history of national banking and of contemporaneous government finance will serve to indicate the train of reasoning by which these conclusions have been arrived at.

Prior to 1878, when the Silver Coinage Act was passed, the evil day which the National Banks felt must eventually come upon them in the extinction of the interest-bearing public debt, appeared to be encouragingly remote. During the six preceding years the reduction of the debt had been about one per cent. for the entire term, a subsidence so gradual as apparently to justify a general consignment to future generations of all fears as to the curtailment of the banking system. But this sense of security was abruptly destroyed. A prosperity unparalleled in its way in the history of the world enabled the country to pay off upwards of 35 per cent. of the debt referred to between 1878 and 1886, thereby spreading grave uneasiness and apprehension among National Banks, feelings which were much accentuated when an official statement by the Comptroller of the Currency gave substance to their own fears by declaring that it was "questioned whether there was power under the Constitution for the Charter of National Banks except as instrumentalities for a money circulation."

This was bad enough; but still, however remote, the liquidation of the national indebtedness had always been a possibility—a certainty indeed—and the National Banks would not have greatly complained of such an adverse turn of fortune if it had come alone. With considerable show of reason they had fostered the impression that they were indispensable to the financial welfare and prosperity of the country. So long as they were recognized as the sole medium of circulation it was inconceivable to them that they should ever cease to exist. They trusted to the Government to devise some means of perpetuating their circulation, even after the last interest bearing bond had been called in; and in the continuance of the circulation they saw the indefinite prolongation of their own term of existence. But to them, as to others, it was the unexpected which happened. In 1878 the Silver Coinage Act was passed, which up to date has resulted in adding $280,000,000 to the country's circulation. In order to insure that there should be no question as to the actual employment of the new silver dollars the right of issue by National Banks of all notes of a lower denomination than $5 was stopped early in 1879. This was a blow in the face to the National Banks. These small notes formed the most desirable part of their circulation. A single dollar note in passing from hand to hand was, in the country where the names on the notes are remarked, the best advertisement any bank could have for the money.

The whole position was becoming irksome as between the Government and the banks ; but the relations of the two were destined to become still further strained. The silver certificates, the issue of which commenced in 1878, rose to $72,000,000 in 1883 and to $145,543,150 in 1887 ; the right of small issue, which the Government had wrested with the strong hand from the National Banks in 1879, was appropriated by it in 1886 and the issue of silver certificates in $1, $2 and $5 then commenced. The effect of the Government issue of silver certificates on the National Banks began to be noticeable in the issues in 1883, and while the former swelled to the proportions stated, the latter's circulation as a consequence, as rapidly decreased. The amount outstanding in 1883 was $311,000,000 ; in 1887, it was $166,000,000.

At this juncture it is well to inquire as to the attitude of the National Banks under this system of spoilage. A glance at their published returns reveals it with tolerable clearness, and it must be confessed that the revelation is an ominous one, more especially when we recollect that it represents the trained intelligence of experienced financiers wielding the greatest monetary influence in this country. The air of disapprobation assumed by the National Banks as seen in their published returns is almost one of menace toward the Government. On June 30th, 1866, the amount of specie held by the National Banks was $12,000,000; according to the latest returns it was $165,000,000, of which immense sum 93 per cent. was represented by gold coin or gold certificates. This ostentatious neglect of the Government silver and silver certificates appears designed as a very pointed rebuke of the course pursued by the Government. No doubt the banks remarked that in the history of Europe, Government interference with a country's circulation had been invariably attended with disastrous results. There was certainly something in the brief nine years experience in this country to suggest the reflection that history was again about to repeat itself.

During the ten years which have elapsed since the silver coinage began the Government has produced $80,000,000 more than had been coined since the organization of the mint in 1793. This step, it was anticipated, would increase the price of silver and would probably consummate the reintroduction of bi-metallism into Europe. It failed conspicuously in both objects. Such a holocaust of the precious metal ought to have done more than merely uphold the figures; it ought to have improved them. Strange, however, to say, it falsified the most modest hopes, as, on the other hand, it is only just to add, it falsified with equal zeal all the expressed fears of those who were opposed to it. The governing quotation in London, which was 55 pence per standard ounce when this stupendous coinage began, retreated, not headlong, but by well considered steps, to 42 pence; or, to put it in intelligible figures, the intrinsic value of the silver dollar, which in February, 1878, when the coinage began, was 93 cents, had by the 31st of July, 1886, fallen to 71 cents; *i.e.*, 29 per cent below its face value. And as for the probabilities of bi-metallism, M. Cernuschi, its champion, has told us with much sadness that America, instead of promoting it by this coinage, "has done the good cause much harm." There was, therefore, some show of reason why prudent bankers should hold aloof while the Government was apparently plunging rashly ahead with its coinage in such a sea of financial fog.

But what does the present attitude of these banks mean? Does it imply that they share in the pessimistic views of the Old World economists that such a divorce between the intrinsic and face value of the silver coin implies sooner or later an appalling dislocation of trade—that the Government is sowing the wind only to reap the whirlwind later on, when the real and artificial values are finally to

be adjusted—that, instead of being comforted by
the fact that the Government has made a profit of
$40,000,000 on the purchase and coinage of silver,
their conservatism is appalled at the idea of this
seignorage item appearing at all in well regulated
Government books? And do they mean to say,
when they eventually speak—"As for your depreciated silver, we will have none of it ; this kind of
thing may suit the Russian peasant and the Indian
ryot, but it won't suit us. Hands off the currency,
gentlemen!" If these are their views, they will
probably have a great many of the thinking people
of the world on their side. They certainly will have
a majority of the political economists of Europe.
Still, even then, they may not be absolutely or even
approximately correct. The United States of America have a habit of upsetting recognized theories ;
and it is evident that in this case, the financial pre-
cepts of the Old World do not consort with the requirements of the New. This country is a law unto
itself, and it is possible, nay, it is even very probable, that in this coinage matter the Government
builded better than they knew and that their very
indiscretion has served them well. It is to be
pointed out that none of the evils usually attrib-
uted to the unlimited use of silver have accrued
therefrom. Even the great London *Economist*, the
most reputable and conservative of financial jour-
nals in Europe, is in full alignment with this idea
when it states in its last issue that " the appre-
hensions which some appear to entertain lest the
freer use of silver in the States shall cause a dete-

rioration of the currency, appear as yet to be groundless.''

Nor need the results of the experiments of European governments in handling their currency daunt us. That the governments of Russia, Austria, Italy, Spain and Turkey should tamper with the national currency and depreciate it has no bearing on the point at all; those are not wealthy countries like this; and in their case the currency was unscrupulously used to eke out failing royal exchequers. As for the seigniorage or profit on the coinage, that cannot be said to afford any reasonable ground for anxiety. If the Government carry this profit into a sinking fund for the benfit of the silver circulation, it is difficult to see any danger in that connection. It is possible, however, that the National Banks attach no importance to these considerations and that their attitude towards the silver circulation of the Government is assumed wholly as an expression of disapproval of acts which appear to threaten their existence. It is probably safe to say that the National Banks are not very closely wedded to their circulation. The profit on it is but small: less than 2 per cent. after deducting the 1 per cent. of annual tax. Every intelligent man knows that it costs him nothing to make his banker his book-keeper as well, and by drawing checks for all amounts over $5, make him bookkeeper and banker in one. In Great Britain, each check bears a penny or 2-cent stamp, which, to the parsimonious man, is somewhat of a drawback. Here checks are free as air, and this fact and many other more

substantial reasons, such as the development of
banking throughout the country, tend to the sup-
planting of large notes by checks. The future of
note circulation is in fact hardly worth considering
from the point of view of pecuniary profit. This is
the more apparent from the fact that in the transaction of its business the percentage of notes and
coin employed by New York is 1.30 against 98.70
of checks and drafts. Probably, however, the
banks parted from their small circulation with regret.
If we may judge from the evidence of foreign banks
they certainly did so. The English banks (outside
of the Bank of England) which cannot issue notes
for a smaller denomination than five pounds, do not
exercise their privilege of circulation to one-half
their legal extent; whereas, the Scotch banks,
which are entitled to issue smaller notes, do so to
an extent double their fixed allowance, keeping gold
on hand against the excess. There are, however,
unmistakable indications of indifference on the
part of the National Banks to their circulation as
such; there are, for instance, in the City of New
York, six banks representing a capital of $10,000,-
000 which have conformed to the legal requirements
as to the deposit of government bonds, but have
either surrendered their issue, or have not considered it worth their while to take it out. Taking
the system as a whole, the National Banks have
availed themselves to the extent of only 32 per cent.
of their authorized issue.

The National Banks thus in semi-revolt against
the Government are disturbed by these thoughts

early dissolution and the satisfaction which they find in noticing the remarkable growth of public confidence, as shown by their increased deposits, is by no means an unmixed joy.

Such is a brief history of the events which have brought about the existing condition of affairs, the main features of which are as follows:

(1.) The existence of a National Banking system representing 3061 establishments, individual deposits to the extent of $1,250,000,000 and, reciprocally, loans and discounts to the public of $1,600,-000,000. This system is firmly entrenched in the confidence of the public; it was organized at a period when the country groaned under a species of financial anarchy and it was mainly instrumental in restoring confidence and in enabling the people to avail themselves of the great capabilities of their land. If this vast growth were a noxious tumor battening on the country's vitals it might possibly be removed without absolute danger; but, as shown by the above figures, it gives more than it receives; and in addition to its functions as a source of supply, it is in truth the very heart itself of the country's trade, feeding, purifying and correcting, as well as commanding, every artery and vein of commerce. As pointed out by the Comptroller of the Currency in his Annual Report for the current year, the aggregate capital, surplus, undivided profits, circulation and deposits have increased from $1,208,781,908 in January, 1866, to $2,240,587,843 in October, 1887, which is less than double, while the loans and discounts have gone up from $500,650,109 to $1,580,045,647, which is more than treble, showing how much more widely the banks are now identified with the general business of the country than 22 years ago. Investments in bonds have taken an opposite course, being less than one-third of what they were in 1879. This system cannot be removed, although it may be and must be reconstructed upon an altered and broader basis, one which will extend and not impair its usefulness.

(2.) National Bank currency, amounting at close of fiscal year to . * $279,217,788

(3.) Government currency issued against credit (Greenbacks) . . 346,681,016

(4.) Gold certificates issued and in Treasury 121,486,817

(5.) Gold coin, deducting next above, ... † 533,033,518

(6.) Silver certificates issued and in Treasury 145,543,150

(7.) Silver coin, deducting next above, and including subsidiary silver, ‡ 207,450,416

(8.) Fractional currency and other items, ... 15,737,210

Total circulation, $1649,149,915

Let us endeavor to anticipate the arguments which will probably be used against an increased circulation, and answer them in advance.

---

* This item includes all outstanding National Bank notes; the amount of circulation of existing banks is $166,000,000.

† Includes $55,512,270 bullion.   ‡ Includes $4,091,414 bullion.

FIRST.—In round numbers, the United States have a total circulating medium of $1,650,000,000 or $27 per head.

Germany $714,000,000
or $16 per head.

Great Britain $895,000,000
or $25 per head.

SECOND. —Relative amount of silver in the United States, including subsidiary silver . $352,000,000
Germany 190,000,000
Great Britain 96,000,000

THIRD.—England has no bank note of smaller denomination than five pounds, or $25. Scotland and Ireland, one pound, or $5. Germany has notes of the value of 5, 20 and 50 marks (*i. e.*, respectively $1.19, $4.76 and $11.90.)

FOURTH.—America does not actually employ a greater proportion of circulation than England. According to official data (1881) the percentage of coin used in London was .73; in New York .55. Of the notes, London uses 2.04, New York .65, while New York employs 98.80 checks and London 97.23. The ratio of coin used in New York has decreased since. Confining the comparison to one country, and that the one which runs most on all fours with our own, the essence of these facts is that the United States have already a total circulation of $754,000,000 in excess of that of Great Britain, including silver circulation three and a half times greater and while possessing a small note currency (in denominations of $1, $2, $5, $10 and $20) which that country does not possess and which ought to remove the necessity for so much silver; furthermore, that New York at least does not make of its silver as much proportionate use as London.

Therefore, the opponents of an extended circulation might say, if Great Britain with its vast volume of trade can work satisfactorily with so moderate a circulation, what a palpable absurdity it is for us to have so large a one. The best reply to which is a demand to know what the standard of circulation is supposed to be based on. On population? so many coins and notes to so many heads? Or by the extent of the country's general trade? Or by the country's wealth? These are factors in the consideration, no doubt, but they are by no means ruling or even important factors. Assuming for the moment that the United States and Great Britain were countries of equal wealth, equal trade, and equal population, ought their circulation to be the same in amount in order to secure equal safety and convenience in business transactions? By no means. A large country can no more be safely secured by a small circulation than an extensive and exposed territory can be adequately protected by a small army in the presence of the enemy. Here is the difference between Great Britain and America. English panics do not extend either to Scotland or Ireland. Therefore, London, where the money is hoarded, is within four hours of every point threatened during a monetary crisis; and the money she hoards is multiplied manifold by its comeatability; it can be removed from point to point to meet the demand, even let the latter sway as widely as it will within the limits of its narrow domain. Credit is older and more solid in Great Britain. And again, London is itself the incubator of all English panics ; the English provinces do not generate them ; so that, unless the panic spreads from London, the latter has only to look out for itself, and as money is drawn out of one bank there, it is put into another, and again immediately available. Here it is entirely different. During panics the danger is regarded with so much alarm that people take money and hoard it in deposit vaults, as Mr. Thompson points out in his interesting pamphlet. Instead of a maximum distance of four hours by rail from the central moneyed point, we have one thirty-six times greater, in addition to a younger and more sensitive credit. All the evil a panic causes is usually wrought within the first 24 hours. At the end of that time the bank has either closed its doors or confidence has been restored. Hence, the necessity of keeping reserves of currency at accessible points over the whole of this vast continent. It would be just as reasonable to say that the currency of this country should be thirty times greater than that of Great Britain because our territory is thirty times larger as to say that it ought only to keep step with our population and commerce to English time. Area and general stability are beyond doubt the great twin-brethren to decide this hard fought question of circulation.

The following extracts from the London *Econo-*

mist will serve to show how little the circulation of any country has to do with the growth of trade and population:

"The note circulation of England and Wales, "instead of expanding in harmony, although not "necessarily in proportion with the increase of "population and growth of trade, has declined."

And the same well known paper proceeds to furnish a table showing as a result that the bank notes in circulation in 1887 were actually less than in 1844. The *Economist* adds:

"When, however, we come to compare circula-"tion with population (*i.e.*, in the English prov-"inces) the diminution assumes very much larger "proportions. In round numbers, the £15,000,000 "of circulation in 1884 was distributed among a "population of about 14,000,000, and thus aver-"aged nearly 21s. 6d. per head, whereas the circu-"lation of £11,300,000 in 1887 was distributed "among a population of about 23,000,000, and "averaged less than 10s. per head."

This country is now probably at that period in its history when it requires its maximum of circulation. The entire area of the country is covered by trade, however sparsely, and needs likewise to be covered by circulation. With the development of commerce, greater transport and increased banking facilities will probably be found to lessen the necessity for so much currency. Meantime, and at this juncture, the writer is disposed to support the assertion made by some able and qualified writers, that a circulation of $2,000,000,000 would be the proper currency equipment of this country.

Turning to the question of the Government issue of silver currency, at which the National Banks appear to glance askance, the writer will endeavor to make his. views on the subject intelligible. We have obviously failed to convert the dull intelligences of Europe to our views on bi-metallism, and if we did not succeed in inducing them to monetize or remonetize silver when we had little of the coin on hand, and accordingly appeared more disinterested than we do at the present time, and when the intrinsic value of the coin approximated to its face value, our case, it is to be feared, would not have appeared to improve in their eyes, were we to say to them now, you *must* remonetize silver because we have so much of it on hand in coin and metal in our vaults and because our coin is only worth 74 cents on the dollar intrinsically. The foreign market, therefore, has certainly not grown more hopeful of recent years. It is, however, dawning upon America that she can live without being much concerned with European bi-metallism. If the Treasury will convert its present willingness to pay for its own silver dollars with gold dollars, into an absolute promise to do so, depreciation ceases once for all. On the basis of such a proposition, the writer makes the following suggestion :

Assuming that neither the population nor the commerce of any country determine its proportionate circulation, (an assumption amply and strikingly justified by the experience of Great Britain, where the circulation does not respond at all to the growth in population or commerce), but that area and the question of established credit are more important factors, it will be fair to assume that the sum of $2,000,000,000 as a circulation would be needed to meet the requirements of this country at all times, including periods of panic. The suggestion then is, establish a circulation as follows :

(1.) A coinage of . . . $2,000,000,000
consisting approximately of 2-3 gold and 1-3 silver, as the basis of a circulating medium, comprising— . . . . .

(2) A paper currency secured by gold . . $800,000,000

(3.) A silver currency payable in gold . 600,000,000

(4.) Gold coin . 600,000,000
_____

$2,000,000,000

(5.) The issue of small notes under $5 to be discontinued and no gold coin less than $5 to be issued.

(6.) The profit on coinage of $600,000,000 silver— which would be upwards of $100,000,000, if the balance of silver requisite to coin that sum were to be bought at current rates (say 74 cents)— if specially invested at 3 per cent. for the benefit of the circulation, would amount at compound interest in 25 years to $209,000,000, and be more than sufficient to make up the par value of the dollar if the Government had eventually to sell the old coins as bullion.

(7.) Assuming the worst imaginable panic, if there were no issue of small notes and no gold coin of less value than $5, this silver circulation *never could be presented for payment* to any extent, as the people would need it for daily use, so that the integrity of the silver dollar would be maintained:—

(a) Because it never could be presented in quantity ;

(b) Because the holder would never apply for gold if he knew he could get it at any time ;

(c) Because the law of averages would always leave enough gold to meet it ; and,

(d) Because the compound interest on the seigniorage would be building up an ample fund to meet any conceivable deficiency.

In passing, the writer would say that such a course would bring the silver coin into the market and subject it to abrasion and loss, which would be better than that it should be rendered immortal by (metaphorically speaking) being wrapped up in tissue paper and stored away in the Treasury vaults. In this suggestion the writer premises that the Government would take the earliest opportunity of providing a metallic basis for its legal tender notes.

Since penning the foregoing suggestions on the currency the writer has noticed the opinion on the same subject of one of the brightest and, most reliable lights that ever illuminated the Treasury Department.

In his Annual Report to Congress, dated 7th December, 1885, the late ex-Secretary Manning says:

"Currency reform is first in the order of importance and of time, and fitly precedes other reforms. . . . . Such a reform of the whole currency of the United States (setting aside the National Bank notes which are diminishing and well secured) can be undertaken and finished subject to the following conditions:

"THE CONDITIONS OF CURRENCY REFORM.

"1. Without shock or disturbance to the industries, the business enterprise, the domestic trade or foreign commerce of the country.

"2. Without degrading the United States monetary unit of value to a cheaper dollar, and without raising the United States monetary unit of value to a costlier dollar.

"3. Without loss to any who now hold the promise of the United States to pay a dollar.

"4. Without reduction of the present volume of the currency, or hindrance to its free increase hereafter, when every dollar note shall be the certificate of a coin dollar in the Treasury payable on demand.

"5. Without pause in the reduction of the public debt, but paying more than three-fifths of all that part of the debt now payable at the option of the United States prior to September, 1891.

"6. Without increase of taxation.

"7. Without the sale of any silver bought and coined since February, 1878.

"8. Without the disuse of the 215,000,000 coined silver dollars of unlimited legal tender, or any fall or discount in their present received value; and without the disuse of the 550,000,000 coined gold dollars of unlimited legal tender, or any rise or premium on their present received value.

"9. Without prejudice to the adoption hereafter of an international bi-metallic union, with free coinage of both metals for all comers, at a fixed ratio of weights, into coin of unlimited legal tender.

"10. Without the coins of the two metals parting company from each other, whatever may be the temporary fall, if any, in the market price of silver bullion after stopping Treasury purchases.

"I would most respectfully commend to the consideration of Congress the question whether such a reform of the currency ought not now to be endeavored; whether these are not among the prudent and just conditions of its reform, and whether such a reform might not be promoted, with immediate advantage to all our industries and trade, by repeal of the clause requiring Treasury purchases of silver bullion, and repeal of the act making compulsory Treasury issues and re-issues of the legal tender notes."

In the writer's judgment, Mr. Manning suggests the only sound, economical and dignified course open to the government of a great country such as this is, when he advises "a currency in which every "dollar note shall be the representative certificate "of a coin dollar actually in the Treasury and pay- "able on demand." He again adds, as if to emphasize its importance, "in which our monetary "unit coined in gold and its equivalent coined in "silver shall not be suffered to part company." The fact that this country was fortified by a circulation such as has been suggested by the writer would be of enormous service to the community in time of international trouble. While designed for the uses of peace it would be better than Germany's military chest in times of war—should such ever arise—and if foreign countries knew that they could always obtain, under any stress of circumstance, a gold dollar in exchange for a silver one, the latter would always remain with them, as a mere token or expression of gold value, so that the gold standard for the silver currency would be maintained in its integrity.

But let us consider the other suggestions made, in and out of Congress.

In his annual report to Congress for the current session the Comptroller of the Currency states that more than forty plans have been proposed to him as a new basis for circulation. These he reduces to five and subsequently to one, when he says that the fifth proposition alone seems to contain a principle likely to be both acceptable and practicably effective. "This principle is, that while preserving "all the other features of the system, the main "volume of the currency should rest upon the

"credit and resources of the banks and not upon
"the credit of the Government, with the reservation
"that whatever new legislation is proposed should
"be additional to, and not in repeal of, existing
"laws as to the deposit of bonds, whether obliga-
"tory or optional, and as to the privilege of issuing
"currency to 90 per cent. of such deposits."

In considering this proposition the Comptroller
alludes to the fact that the proposed issue of notes
would constitute a first lien upon all the assets of a
failed bank and draws attention to the difference
between such a lien and that at present exacted by
the Government, which is a security for only the
deficiency between the proceeds of the deposited
bonds and the outstanding circulation, a deficiency
which has never occurred and, in the present state
of the market for United St.tes bonds, is not likely
to arise. He accentuates the fact that the preference thus secured to note-holders over depositors
of the National Banks has never been enforced and
its legal existence has never affected the general
credit of these institutions. In the case, however,
of an issue not specially secured, which in the
event of insolvency must be redeemed wholly out
of the general assets, the effect caused by the existence of such a lien must affect unfavorably the
minds of depositors. In this relationship he refers
to the enormous amount of individual deposits in
the National Banks which would be influenced by
any such prior lien given to the note-holders. Few
people will be disposed to question the correctness

of his deductions as reported in the following
words :

"The issue of preferred notes to the amount of even 25 per
cent. of the capital, the lowest limit proposed, would be a serious
matter to depositors, while such issues to the amount of 50, 75,
and 100 per cent. of capital, as some suggest, would probably
cripple fatally the general credit of the banks with prudent
depositors, and in that way their means of accommodation
would be curtailed in a ratio greater than the increase of such
means derived from the additional issues of currency. It is
much more important to the banks as a body to retain and
augment their deposits than to acquire the power to issue more
currency, and the public have even a greater interest than the
banks in the preservation of this condition of things, because
the credit that attracts deposits is always better founded than
that which floats currency, and is always more jealously guarded
by the banks enjoying it, and it is, therefore, less liable to be
abused. The conclusion reached is fatal to all schemes of estab-
lishing a bank currency secured only by a first lien upon all the
assets of the issuing bank, unless some sufficient counterpoise to
the objections can be found among the various suggestions as
to a 25 per cent. reserve, a sinking fund deposited with the
Government, the consolidation of all issuing banks into one
association, &c."

One of the best conceived plans in advocacy of
the circulation based on credit which the writer
has seen is that suggested in his pamphlet by Mr.
John Thompson, Vice-President of the Chase National Bank, who is recognized as an able authority
on such subjects. Mr. Thompson's plan is briefly
that the banks should discontinue the deposit of
Government bonds as security for currency—should
be empowered to obtain currency from the Treasury
Department equal to fifty per cent. on their paid up
capital, such issue to have a preferred lien on the
entire assets of the bank, including the individual

liability of the stockholders in case of insolvency,
and that the annual internal revenue tax of one per
cent. per annum on circulation be converted into a
guarantee fund for the benefit of the currency.   In
support of his views, Mr. Thompson quotes extracts
from the report to the Congress of 1885 by the then
Comptroller of the Currency, Hon. H. W. Cannon,
now President of the Chase National Bank.   Ex-
pressions from such influential authorities in favor
of a credit currency are entitled to full consideration, and it is with some degree of diffidence that
the writer ventures to criticise them.   The one stu-
pendous disadvantage of an issue based on the
credit of individual banks lies in the fact that, for
one central source of issue of the circulating medium of the country as it at present exists in the
United States Government, it proposes to substitute
a large number of small establishments of issue
which already amount to upwards of 3000, and
would in time probably amount to 10,000.   When
the enormous territory covered by these banks is
taken into consideration and the terrific onslaught
reasonably to be expected on them during a period
of acute panic, it must be admitted that the pros-
pect of the formation of such a long, thin line of
units of issue of irregular strength is nothing short
of appalling ; more particularly when it is remem-
bered that a single failure would bring discredit
upon all issues, and probably convert the objec-
tionable line into a row of ninepins, where the fall
of one would endanger the standing of all.   The
integrity of such a conglomeration of issues, it

must be confessed, would be likely to compare very unfavorably with the security of the existing currency emanating from—and not only guaranteed, but in extremity payable, by—the Government which holds against it what is tantamount to cash.

It is very conceivable that any Government would shrink from the vastly increased responsibility involved in the inspection of banks which have changed from a cash to a credit circulation with its additional exposure to discredit and its attendant dangers from overtrading.

From the depositor's point of view there are also grave objections to this currency-upon-credit system, which means that the National Banks shall, at the outset, be saddled with a first mortgage, and that both stockholders and depositors shall in future assume greater risks in banking ; for cipher it as one may, it is impossible to add from two to three hundred million dollars to the currency of a country on credit and not materially increase the risks of the banking system responsible for it. Upon investigation too, this proposition, while designed to ensure the safety of the circulating notes and in reality weakening the position of the depositors and stockholders in order to do so, does not materially help the note-holder. Let it be assumed, for instance, that a rumor were to arise affecting the credit of a note-issuing bank in a populous center, and it is quite safe to say that the bulk of the depositors would have caught the alarm and have withdrawn their money, clearing out the bank in the process, before even the first holder of a note had discovered that he had one in his possession ; and it would be just as bad for him to have the value of his notes locked up awaiting the liquidation of the bank, as if he were a depositor.

In a country town where there are only one or two banks of issue, the difference between each bank's notes is remarked ; whereas, in large cities, it is never noticed. Therefore, this proposition may be said to increase the risks of the depositors and stockholders by tending towards overtrading by means of a first lien, which, while designed to benefit the holder of the mortgage or bank note, does not really do so, as, for the reasons assigned, it enables the depositor to obtain an advantage over him as long as the bank can pay cash.

The very important feature of the surrender of the Government tax of one per cent. for the establishment of a note guarantee fund would no doubt go far to obviate the danger of loss to the stockholders, though not to remove the stigma which the failure of one bank would still entail to the entire system. The number of National Banks which failed last year was eight, the average for the last four years was the same.

It is clear that if this average was maintained, as it is certain to be, we should have banks whose notes were discredited (at the outset even if paid eventually) during the first year of the new arrangement. The Government, however, which has all along had its one per cent. on the circulation,

and has, it must be confessed, well earned it, would
not consent to a surrender of it *in toto*. It is not
reasonable to suppose that any Government should
agree to exercise so wide, so exacting, and so responsible a censorship over a wealthy body, and
run the risk of showing a loss resulting therefrom
to the department exercising the supervision. It
is indeed very intelligible that a careful Government should impose a tax such as would bring a
fair share of revenue since the banks have really no
more right to make a profit out of circulation than
any other commercial enterprises have. The profit,
if any, belongs to the people or to their representative, the Government. And here it is to be
remarked that the present Comptroller suggests
a modification of the tax. The necessity for such
a modification is not very apparent, but the possibility of it indicates a weakness of one of the props
on which Mr. Thompson's proposed fabric was to
be built. In all the circumstances of the case it is
hardly possible to conceive that Congress will
emasculate this tax to any extent, even for such a
desirable purpose as the formation of a fund to
guarantee the note issue ; and there is the danger
that, even if the Government agreed to the proposition, a panic might exhaust the fund in its infancy when it is quite safe to say that the holders'
delay in realizing as the first creditor would be almost as ruinous as a total loss ; for the delay in
payment during panic is as bad as actual loss.

On the surface of this proposition too, lies this
difficulty : Is it not calculated to restrain freedom

in banking ? Assuming, for instance, that the National Banks in existence had built up a guarantee fund of say $5,000,000, upon what principle, if any, would they be prepared to allow new banks admission into the fund ?

The Hon. John Jay Knox's proposition was the accumulation of a safety fund, first from the gain arising from the accidental loss or destruction of the circulating notes of National Banks ; second, from the tax upon the circulation ; and third, from interest to be derived at a low rate upon the fund on deposit in the treasury for the purpose of reducing notes of National Banks retiring circulation, which now amounts to $39,000,000. The amount available for a safety fund from the first source was estimated in 1885 to be not less than $6,000,000 ; and the amount derived from the tax for safety fund taxes, even if fixed at one-half per cent., in the course of three years, the safety fund on hand would amount to more than $10,000,000.

While this plan appears to suggest good security, it has the disadvantage, already alluded to, of limiting the freedom of banks to be formed subsequently.

Mrs. Glass's well known recipe for cooking a certain rodent—"first catch your hare"—would appear to be applicable here, since it is very doubtful indeed if the National Banks would be permitted to avail themselves of any of these funds.

Apparently the most popular as well as the most recent suggestion is the proposition to make the issuance of bank notes optional with the banks themselves and to maintain the latter's relations with the Government by the deposit of a nominal sum (say $1,000) with the Treasury. Of this it may be said that if Government supervision is absolutely imperative, and a device is necessary to maintain it, this is probably as good as any other.

But why this undesirable air of "tinkering" this currency problem? Why not go direct to Congress and obtain the needful powers compelling Government supervision, if such is desirable? As already expressed, the writer does not think that it is—but on the contrary protests that it is un-business-like and unconstitutional. It is time the National Banks were out of the Government's leading strings, which, however needful once, are no longer necessary now. Circumstances are already cutting away these evidences of infancy, and it would better consort with the dignity of the banks to let them go without demur.

It seems to the writer that the National Banking system has now reached a stage when Government supervision is not only unnecessary but harmful, both to the banks themselves and to the public. To the banks, because once they have passed the very superficial scrutiny of the official examiner, the directors and officers are prone to think that all is well, and to relax their vigilance and so fall short of that degree of excellence of management which it is possible they might attain to if their standard were a higher, or a rising, one ; because, also, they grow to lean upon the Government, and are apt to lose that courage of conviction, and prompt decision of judgment which are as necessary to a banker as ceaseless watchfulness and uniform prudence. How many directors have neglected their duties, using the Government Inspector as a sentinel to notify danger, and intensifying their neglect with every round which he completed without an alarm being sounded? One very common instance of the harm likely to result to the banks under such supervision will suffice. If a banker has any transaction on his books as to the safety or propriety of which he is doubtful, and if that transaction is passed by the Examiner without comment, the fact that it has so been passed will either lessen the just doubts of the banker as to its safety and so breed a degree of confidence unwarrantable in the circumstances, or, in the case of an irregularity, embolden him to increased acts of banking impropriety.

The moral effect of an official examination is rarely negative—and nearly always positive—distinctly baneful if not manifestly beneficial.

It is hurtful to the public because the latter regard the official inspection as a Government endorsement of each individual bank—a clean bill of health, equally free from fraud and mismanagement,—a perfectly monstrous idea when the superficial character of the examination is considered, and a grotesque one when the long continued iniquities which cause so many bank failures are borne in mind.

There comes a time when it is necessary to take away his crutches from the invalid in order to ensure that he regains the full and perfect use of his limbs, and the present appears a favorable hour in which to perform that ceremony for the National Banks.

In saying this no shadow of aspersion is cast on those who introduced this supervision as a corollary to the National Banking system. It will indeed be seen by the following quotation from the Report (Dec. 1887) of the Comptroller of the Currency that the original design of those who insisted upon it was widely different from what it is commonly supposed to have been.

"It would appear that the supervision of the National banks by the Comptroller of the Currency was intended originally only to protect the Revenue from being defrauded and the public from suffering loss through improper issues of circulating notes, but in process of time the supervision came to be extended so as to serve as a protection to depositors against the maladministration of Directors ; and *quite recently* it has been assumed that Examiners are expected to discover the defalcations of cashiers and tellers, fraudulent entries in the books of banks, and false statements of assets and liabilities in cases where the President and Directors or some of them have failed to make such discoveries."

Then follows this momentous paragraph.

"However desirable it may be that examiners should be encouraged to fulfil this extreme expectation, *yet no one of practical experience would rely upon an Examiner who comes only once a year and who can afford to stay but a single day to discover thefts or false entries, that have been successfully concealed from Directors who are always present, and whose money is being stolen.* All efforts must be futile that are directed to supplying by means of official examination an effective substitute for the vigilance and personal accountability of directors. Legislative or administrative force applied to such efforts will be misapplied and wasted."

The italics are in each instance the writer's. From the foregoing it will be seen that the Government altogether deprecate being considered as Bank Inspectors in the current acceptation of the term, and that they rather indeed resent the anomalous if not actually false position in which public estimate has wrongly placed them, not always but "*quite recently.*" Their care, it would appear, was not originally in reference to the safety of the deposits or public money, but to the circulation as to the safety of which no one had ever any manner of doubt.

The Comptroller disclaims all responsibility as to the honesty and efficiency of the interior administration of National Banks, and very justly casts on the President and directors the sole responsibility of all fraud and irregularities in connection therewith. His functions, he goes on to say, do not extend beyond the ascertainment that the bank is properly organized and administered, and that "No law has "been violated in respect to loans, reserve, invest- "ments, bad debts, or dividends; and that the "assets are really worth the amounts representing "them on the books of the bank."

That this system of inspection has been of some efficacy is undoubted; inasmuch as it has inculcated sound banking principles; but for all purposes of detecting fraud on the part of directors or officers it might as well be conducted with a foot rule, and the assets be assessed according to their cubic dimensions. There is absolutely no protection in it against fraud which has passed the rudimentary stage.

In such circumstances the public ought not to be found inconsolable at the bereavement if the Government Examiners are taken from them. It is evident that however efficient for the purposes for which they were designed, they were, and are, and cannot help continuing to be, broken reeds, as far as public confidence is concerned.

It ought not to have been left to the present Comptroller of the Currency to define the Government's position in this matter a quarter of a century after the first dawning of misapprehension was apparent. No Government having a due regard to its honor ought to permit itself to be placed erroneously and without public and reiterated protest on its part, in a seemingly fiduciary relationship towards the people, and more particularly in any connection involving the risks of trade.

Were the Government well advised, it would take the earliest opportunity of retiring from a position already burdened with weighty responsibilities and destined to be saddled with many more with the growth of banking throughout the country. It is indeed quite inconceivable that the Government should continue its examinations if credit should become the future basis of note issue. Such a course would entail the risk of much odium as well as responsibility.

This subject of Government examination is touched upon elsewhere in these pages, but it may be stated here without fear of contradiction, that however beneficial it may have been in some respects—and in the compilation of rules for the management of these banks it has been invaluable—the official inspection in this country has not guarded the interests of the banks as safely as the automatic and continuous systems of examination conducted in other countries have protected the banks under their eyes.

Experience has demonstrated, times without end, that so far as the depositors were concerned the official examiners have only cleaned the outside of the platter, unconscious of the corruption which has occasionally here and there been growing inside. Colossal frauds have flourished under such inspectors with absolute impunity, and it would be hard to say that all the banks to whom the examiner has given a clean bill of health, as free from fraud or mismanagement, are justly entitled to it.

But therein lies our error; the Comptroller affirms, as quoted, that he never intended to give a clean bill of health, as the public understood it.

It is quite safe to say that the National Banks as a class are worthy of every confidence ; the measure of their support proves that ; but if any man deposits his money in them or increases his deposit because of the Government supervision, it is possible that he might not be able to show much reason for the faith that is in him. The National Bank, governed by present rules, would, in every respect, be as worthy of public confidence without Government supervision as with it.

With reference to the general features of these institutions sufficient praise can scarcely be bestowed upon the wisdom which framed the laws governing the National Banking system. In such a crucial question, for instance, as the legal reserves, this is a particularly noticeable feature. These are, in New York, 25 per cent. of deposits in cash; in other reserve cities, one-half reserve in cash; and in States and Territories the reserve is fixed at fifteen per cent. of which two-fifths must be in cash in the bank. What the laws have compelled in the United States, experience has brought about in England, and the whole theory of both the written laws here and the unwritten laws there is that panics being city born, demand a greater proportion of cash in business centers, although to the inexperienced it might seem natural that new and unsettled districts, where credit is more precarious, would exact a larger proportion of cash on hand.

Similar evidences of experience and forethought are conspicuous both in the restrictions imposed upon the national banks and also upon the management of the banks by their officials. But the certainty of an impending change induces the question " Have we the best form of bank ? and, if so, is it as perfect as it might be?" It would be no reflection on the action of those who so wisely designed the National Banking system in 1863-4, were improvements upon that system to be suggested now after a lapse of a quarter of a century. At the period of its inception the financial sky was dull and lowering, the financial sea was so rough as to threaten to engulf any craft, and the National Banking system, then launched as a lifeboat, did its work well and nobly.

Now, however, the sky is clear and the waters smooth, and what we want now is, that while retaining the principle of the lifeboat, our banking craft should be more of a commercial boat. It is hardly conceivable that government inspection of the National Banks will continue after the note circulation ceases, as, however desirable in founding a system, it is no more a function of the Government to inspect banks than it is their duty to inspect the books of any other commercial organization. As, therefore, the bank of the future will, in all probability, require to depend on itself for inspection, the question arises whether other countries can teach us anything on this subject. The writer assuredly thinks that Great Britain can; and he would suggest for the consideration of those interested, the subject of the joint stock banking system, which has stood the test so well in England and Ireland during the last half century and in Scotland for nearly two centuries. Instead of isolated establishments as in this country, that system consists of parent establishments with numerous branches. As the national banking system stands at present, it has the following drawbacks as compared with the joint stock system of Great Britain:

First. The banks are isolated establishments, mere monoliths, and many of them are too small to stand any special strain. For instance, on the 5th of October, 1887, out of 3049 banks in existence, there were no fewer than 2150 of which the capital did not exceed $150,000, although aggregating the vast total of $179,849,390.

Second. Over eighty per cent. (5,034,325 shares out of 5,731,725) of the stock of these banks is held by residents of the State in which the bank is located. Thus, it will be seen that during a period of local depression in any particular district, the strain would fall upon both stockholders and depositors of the same bank, and so render the crisis doubly acute. If a general depression were known to impair the responsibility of many of the stockholders in a bank which was itself a sufferer by it, the fact would injure the standing of the bank ; and if the initiative were given by any other cause, such knowledge might precipitate its downfall. Then again, the stock of that vast aggregate of small banks has only a local market, which means a limited demand and a relatively low market value in proportion to its dividend earning capacity ; whereas, if the sum named, $179,849,390, were the capital of a few large, well known establishments, and the stock were quoted on the leading exchanges of the country, it would enlarge competition for it enormously and enable the latter to leap to higher figures at once. This is very apparent in the proportion of market price to dividend of the shares of large English banks and of small American banks.

Third. Even in the case of the large National Banks in the cities of this country the market value of their stock is not relatively so high as in Great Britain ; just as in that country the shares of a smaller joint stock bank, however sound, are not so much sought after and do not attain to so high a figure as those of the largest banks. Here it may be stated that the largest national bank in this country scarcely equals in extent of assets the smallest joint stock bank in London. The public stockkholder likes a large bank ; he sees more elbow room in it ; more margin in case of a panic, and apart from that, every force fights for the "big battalions." There is also this fact to be considered —the larger and more widely placed a banking shareholding constituency is, the more likely is a freer and healthier criticism of the published accounts to result than there would be if entirely under local influence. There is more power in proportion in a large bank, more cohesiveness and concentration of action. A large conservative bank tends to keep the stock market steady and to restrain the action of speculative monopolists. And where there is no semi-government bank like the Bank of England or Bank of France, the necessity for large banks during periods of crisis is increased.

Fourth. One of the most serious drawbacks to the national banking system and the cause of a great porportion of the losses and discredit which has fallen upon it from time to time through the defalcations of its officers, is the personal element in the banks. Small local banks are usually formed by a coterie of friends and as a rule in selecting the President, Directors, Cashiers, and Tellers, preference is given to some valued friends or to some relations. Nothing would seem more natural and yet nothing is more absolutely fatal to the welfare of a bank, than to import friendship or, still worse, relationship, into the working of it. As a rule it means inexperience in business; it means unfamiliarity with the temptations arising from the control of much cash; it leads on the one side to remissness in supervision and too often on the other to a tendency to yield under trial and to trust in the event of discovery to the clemency of friends in the same concern.

The returns of banking failures for 1886 are note worthy as affording evidence of the justice of these remarks. Of eight failures, five are owing to fraud or embezzlement by this personal element, and the other three are the result of gross ignorance of the true principles of banking. All the failures are evidently the consequence of an improper selection of officers, probably owing to undue personal bias.

The returns for 1887 are equally suggestive. The number of National Banks which failed is identical with that of the previous year, and the causes are as follows: 1st. President irregularly made use of Bank for his own enterprises. 2d. Bank failed through decline of local business. 3d. Fraud by directors. 4th. Involved with directors in cattle business. 5th. Cashier absconded. 6th. Wrecked by president, who also absconded. 7th. Gross weakness and mismanagement by cashier, and neglect of duty by directors. 8th. Embezzlement by cashier. It is probably safe to say that each of these failures could have been avoided by proper automatic inspection, such as is exercised over their Branches by London Banks.

Of the failures—100 in number—since the establishment of the National Banking system, 63 have have been attributable in whole or in part to ignorance and to loose methods of business.—(Vide Compt. Rept., 1887.)

Banking discipline ought to be of more than Spartan severity ; it unquestionably is so in the large joint stock banks of Great Britain. Perhaps the most notable feature in connection with these joint stock banks is their system of inspection. It is difficult to conceive anything more perfect ; and it is the distilled result of bitter experience. The returns which each branch sends up to its chief office weekly are of the most exhaustive kind and they are scrutinized with eagle eyes by the inspector's staff there. The bills discounted during the week are forwarded to the chief office each Saturday, where they are held. The branches communicate with each other in the receipt and transmittal of moneys only through the central office, thereby enabling the latter to keep full track of every transaction between the two. Twice or three times a year the inspectors from the central office arrive and examine the bank down to its smallest transaction. No notice is given of this intended visit, which usually lasts three days. From daily official letters, from the weekly returns and from previous visits and reports, the inspectors have become familiarized with the business of each branch and the training of a lifetime gives them incredible powers of memory and marvellous instincts for the discovery of any irregularities. This is the perfection of inspection. It goes on without intermission and yet unharrassingly, since it is the acknowledged custom ; and after all is but part of the day's work. Prior to its complete adoption, English joint stock banks suffered cruelly from defalcations; since its perfection, thirty years ago, the great London and provincial joint stock banks have not suffered an appreciable loss through the dishonesty of their employès. Could anything more be said in favor of a system ? But in such organizations no untrained man could make any headway. Principles have to be absorbed not crammed ; and those of banking are of such slow growth as to strain the capacity of a single generation to teach them adequately ; they ought almost to be hereditary. Like the Roman Gladiator, the London banker is unequalled in his profession, but apt to be incapable outside of it. The one transcendent fact which he learns early and never forgets is that ''locked-up'' or unavailable money is only equal to ''lost'' money in his hour of need and he never loses his grip of the situation, or sight of his cash.

In glancing over the official returns of the Comptroller of the Currency, one extraordinary feature, the consideration of which is apart from the object of this paper but still worthy of notice here, is noticeable in connection with national banks, viz. : that no fewer than 52,963 shares in these banks are held by religious, charitable and educational institutions ; and 467,173 by savings banks, trust and insurance companies ; none of these bodies ought to invest in any such securities where a liability is attaching, and the institutions named ought not to retain the risk for an hour ; similar mistakes have worked much havoc elsewhere.

The most familiar and approved form of existing bank in Great Britain is the joint stock bank with a central office in the Metropolis, or other leading city of England, Scotland or Ireland, with branches throughout the country, but usually within a convenient radius of the head office. Some of these banks affect a wider area than others ; the London and County Bank, for instance, with 165 branches and assets of $172,166,107, does not extend its radius further than sixty miles beyond London ; whereas the National Provincial Bank, with 159 branches and assets of $188,530,458, covers all England. With the exception of Scotch banks with London offices, and one Irish bank, the joint stock banks of Great Britain confine their operations to the special country of their adoption ; for instance, English banks do not cross the Scottish border. The branches of these banks are quite as large as the average individual banking institutions of this country. During the past half century these banks have, bit by bit, absorbed the greater number of private banks which occupied the field before they arrived, and although the large private banks of Lombard street, and later on, the old-fashioned West End houses, will all no doubt register under the limited liability act, as Glyn Mills & Co., with their sixty million dollars of assets have done in recent years, and so conformed to public taste and perpetuated their own existence, it is doubtful whether in provincial towns **many** private banks will outlive the century.

The leading private banks of the West End of London, as well as some on the East side of Temple Bar, are of considerable antiquity; they are supported by a clientèle of landed proprietors, removed for the most part from the risks of trade from which they themselves also hold aloof. They discount no commercial paper, and as their patrons have an abiding faith in them and are not at all of a nervous character, they have always looked serenely down upon panics, even when Lombard St. was tottering, as on mere mercantile ebullitions or idiosyncrasies which, although very interesting no doubt, were something with which they had really nothing in the world to do. These banks are *sui generis;* their number is very small—scarcely half a dozen —and very soon they will be the only landmarks left of the once great private banking fabric of England, swallowed up absolutely by the omnivorous joint stock, many-roofed, and omnipotent system. It would have taken another century for that system to have absorbed them if it had not owned branches. A moving population it has been found leaves with one accord its deposits with the bank whose name it already knew in its own town and recognized as a friend in the new, and to it, strange city of its adoption. The manager of one branch simply passes on his client to his brother manager in the new city selected by the client. People do not as a rule think enough of these considerations.

The total deposits in the banks of the United Kingdom are computed at about $2,800,000,000, of which about $2,250,000,000 are held by the joint stock banks of England, Scotland and Ireland. In England, where the absorption of private banks is going on, the deposits of the joint stock banks have increased forty per cent. since 1880.

The total subscribed capital of the joint stock banks of the United Kingdom is now $1,164,762,180, upon which there is paid up $337,940,100, or an average of about 29 per cent. The relatively high price of Bank shares, notwithstanding a liability (uncalled) of 71 per cent., is remarkable.

There is in these joint stock banks the exclusion of the personal element noticeable in the National Banks, and already referred to. So much importance is attached to this that English joint stock banks now make it an invariable rule to appoint their managers only from their regular staff. In the earlier days of the system when competition with private banks was still strong, it was not unusual for the directors in London to give the appointment of manager in a provincial town to some local magnate of recognized wealth and prominent position in order to secure business and to fight the personal influence of the private banks with the personal influence of their new managers; but it was not found to work well as a rule and the practice was abandoned. The invariable rule now is to give such appointments to gentlemen who have graduated in their own office and have been strictly trained in banking discipline. There is an immense advantage in the British system of taking a boy from school or college into the office and letting him adopt banking as a definite career at the outset. All good banks afford liberal pensions to their officers after reasonable service, and it is a great inducement to faithful service to know that if his business life has been spent in one establishment the banking official will be able to retire on a pension equal to two-thirds of his salary when he is very little past middle life. It is safe to say that the officer who began the business as a boy and has been familiarized with the control of money all his life, feels few of the temptations to embezzle which assail a man brought into tempting contact with large funds for the first time in his life. But there are innumerable technical advantages in the British system; in the freedom and sympathy with which a well trained staff work, in the perfecting of a uniform system of bookkeeping and in the formation of useful rules and regulations.

Conspicuous among the advantages of this system is that of safety. Instead of its branches being a source of danger in times of local depression they are the reverse. The other portions of the establishment fly to the assistance of any endangered branch; and even if every dollar invested locally had been lost by the bank the loss would hardly be felt. Indeed it is quite safe to say that there are joint stock banks in Great Britain that could individually lose the total assets of half a score of their branches, without even passing a dividend.

The English bank is enabled to locate its branches

where most suitable in order to form a perfect whole, so that the borrowing element will not greatly exceed the depositing, and so that it may arrange that one class of its customers may deposit at that season of the year when another borrows.

The question then occurs—are such banks profitable? and if so, to what extent? In the report of the Comptroller of the Currency for 1885, a comparison was made between the dividends paid by some of the national banks of this country and certain foreign banks. The capital of the national banks united amounted to $523,-749,658, upon which the average dividend paid was 7.9 per cent. The capital of the British banks amounted to $306,901,203 and the average dividend to 12.4 per cent. The capital of the foreign banks was $454,453,267, and the average dividend they paid was 9.3; by which it will be seen that notwithstanding the higher rate of interest prevailing here the banks of this country are not so remunerative to their shareholders as those of other countries. It is also noticeable that the sixteen London and partly provincial banks which yielded the largest average dividend, namely 14½ per cent. had no circulation to profit by.

The following synopsis of 50 of the principal British joint stock banks will furnish some useful information on that subject; the information, which is the latest available, has been carefully extracted by the writer from the London *Economist* and other reliable papers. In the first four classifications the banks are arranged by sevens to aid in comparing totals and results.

SYNOPSIS OF 50 BRITISH JOINT STOCK BANKS.

Number of Banks.	Where Located.	No. of Branches.	Assets. £	Average Dividend.	Paid up Capital. £	Market Value of Paid up Capital. £	Cash in hand money at call & short notice. £	Res'v fund div. and undivided profits. £	Ratio of reserve to paid up capital. £
7	London Joint Stock Banks.	63	83,930,939	10.6	8,905,000	21,845,000	19,315,220	5,325,507	59.8
7	Lon. and Provincial ditto	562	171,773,027	13.7	20,930,500	67,372,200	41,095,592	7,381,266	35.2
7	Scotch Banks - -	811	97,605,517	12.7	8,250,000	21,375,500	17,729,645	5,179,408	62.7
7	Irish Banks - - -	359	46,970,625	11.7	6,221,288	14,542,800	6,675,500	2,944,955	47.3
22	English Provinc'l J. S. B'ks	586	108,093,124	15.7	9,672,587	29,614,700	19,397,507	7,165,769	74.0
50		2,381	508,373,232	64.4	53,979,375	154,732,200	104,213,464	27,996,905	279.0
			Average, 12.9						Average, 55.8

Omitting the Chemical, First, and Mechanics' National Banks, and the National Broadway Bank, the average dividend of fifteen of the leading National Banks in New York is 8.86 per cent. per annum, and average market value is as 198 to the par value of 100, while the surplus is equal to 63.38 per cent. of the paid up capital. The average paid up capital is $2,013,333 and average surplus $1,276,153. National Bank capital is apparently kept small in some instances to avoid taxation. The average market value of British shares, according to foregoing table, is 286, or 186 premium, as compared with 98 premium in the United States Banks. The average assets of the former is $49,413,875 (say fifty million dollars), and the average paid up capital upwards of $5,000,000 ($5,246,792.) The average of reserve funds, dividends, and undivided profits is $2,721,298, equal to 55.8 per cent. of paid up capital, large though the latter is.

These British banks carry as a whole a larger proportion of share liability than American banks, and the high price at which their shares stand is additionally noteworthy in view of the greater responsibility.

It will be seen from the high *average* of their reserves (2¾ million dollars) and of their cash in hand at call and short notice (10 million dollars additional) that such banks could stand without injury a strain that would wreck a considerable number of small National Banks. This is of great importance, as no epidemic is so contagious as a panic among banks. The mere suspicion of weakness in a small bank may, in times of sensitive credit, extend in an incredibly short time to its neighbors, and gathering both volume and momentum as it goes, soon endanger the strongest bank. This infection of distrust is so well known and recognized among experienced British bankers that it is on record that during one of the few panics with which Scotland has been affected, while one bank was experiencing a sharp "run," the other banks at once and privately carried back to it the funds which its depositors had drawn from it and deposited with them; an act of the soundest policy, for had that bank closed its doors the shock, it is possible, would have shut theirs too.

The writer desires it to be understood that in extolling the British system of bank inspection reference is only made to London banks with metropolitan and provincial branches, where outlying establishments, under the control of managers, and only inspected at intervals from the central office, rendered vitally necessary, at an early stage in their existence, the inauguration of the most perfect known form of bank inspection and the most complete system of weekly reports to act in conjunction therewith.

Banks located elsewhere in Great Britain are no doubt excellently managed in respect of their inspections, but it is probable that none reach the very high standard perfected and maintained in the English metropolis, although doubtlessly copied originally from the more ancient Scottish Joint Stock Banks.

The question will very naturally arise, But who inspects the inspectors?—who examines the chief office which is so supernaturally careful about its branches? The reply to which inquiry is, the corps of inspectors are at work all the time at the chief office when not engaged outside, and they overhaul the books there just as remorselessly as at the smallest branch. It would be a good deal like burglariously entering a prison to attempt fraud at the headquarters of the banking detective system. The moral influence is valuable too, because even the most inconsistent of chairmen or directors would scarcely have the hardihood to submit to his co-directors a business transaction for his own aggrandisement, such as himself and colleagues had been in the habit of condemning in the most unqualified way when proposed by a branch manager. The maxim that "Law makers must not be law breakers" is very strictly observed among British bank directors.

There is also this further safeguard. At the end of each half year the accounts and vouchers of the banks are examined by two or more auditors chosen by the shareholders at public meeting, and these gentlemen are invariably of a position entirely above suspicion. Their scrutiny of the books, vouchers, and securities at the chief office is close and searching, and since they are as a rule professional accountants and auditors they are little likely to be hoodwinked.

It is a comparatively easy matter to unsettle a fraction of the public faith in any undertaking or system; but to do so without being able to suggest something better the writer holds to be a very questionable proceeding.

This paper has already far exceeded its intended limits, and the writer will therefore make his concluding suggestions as briefly as possible.

The National Banking system, it has been pointed out, is firmly established in the confidence of the people, *ergo* it must stay. Under amended conditions, however. This country has no semi-Government banks, like the leading countries of Europe, and on that account, as well as on others, the banking mould must be enlarged. The writer claims some slight experience of panics. He graduated in a leading Scotch bank, was present in the bankers' department of the Bank of England on Black Friday, 1866, when Overend & Gurney failed, and Lombard Street seemed bodily tottering. As all the bankers who required to draw money were represented in that department it formed a perfect thermometer of the conditions outside. The scene of tumult in that usually noiseless chamber was indescribable. The smallest sum asked for—or rather shouted for amid the din —was one hundred thousand pounds in notes (half a million dollars). The writer also passed through the British panic of 1874 as a London bank manager, and his experience, gleaned then and during seventeen years of banking, convinced him of the tremendous superiority of large banks over small ones. There are some Joint Stock Banks in existence in London at the present time which could not be broken by a panic, because they have more money at command than all their tellers could pay away with both hands in three days, and the "run" has yet to be experienced that can last so long in the face of prompt cash.

To the writer it appears inevitable that if the National Banks do not adopt the system of branches they will be swallowed up by some organization which will be established to occupy the field in the way the Joint Stock Banks have occupied Great Britain. The private banks of that country, which half a century ago did all the banking in the British Isles, met the requirements of the public fully as well as the National Banks meet America's necessities to-day. They were free from all suspicion of fraility, there was no lack of confidence in them, no circulation of depreciated value connected with them to tarnish their fair fame; the people, the most conservative in the world, were wedded to the system which under the same names and conditions their fathers and grandfathers had approved and believed in like a creed; and altogether the private banks seemed to be an imperishable institution. But they stood, as the National Banks stand to-day, mere local units without cohesion or combination, and they experienced the fate of all such when fighting against powerful federate action. There came a time eventually, when they were converted to the creed of their great opponents—"*vis unita fortior*" (strength united is stronger)—but it was too late, their fate was sealed, and they could only beg the Joint Stock Banks to absorb them, which the former incontinently did, with such gusto indeed that one bank whose assets now amount to $190,000,000 is said to have swallowed some 300 of them.

America presents to-day the finest field in the world for banking enterprise, and there is untold wealth in its development. This field belongs by right of prior occupancy to the National Banks. Let them assert their claims and adapt themselves to the exigencies of the hour. Let them abandon all claims to note issue, all weak yearnings after Government supervision. Let them amalgamate or consolidate, let them enlarge their foundations and the scope of their operations, let them have branches. There are very few things now remaining in which it is safe to say, "Let the United States copy England in that," and the number grows smaller, but the writer declares, advisedly and without hesitation, that the banking system of that country is the finest product in it, and is a century ahead of the rest of Europe. The writer further thinks that in its cardinal features and general conduct it is entitled to be diligently studied by the bankers of the United States.

In the writer's judgment, if this country had 100 large banks with numerous branches, it would be much better for the financial safety of the country than if its banking was entrusted to 3,000 small and separate banks. Large banks do not become monopolists, on the contrary, they have proved to be foils to monopoly, and to be a reliable means of steadying the market.

This country beyond all doubt needs such banks with central offices in New York, Philadelphia, Boston, Chicago, St. Louis, San Francisco and other leading cities, and with branches radiating from such central points to a distance of from 300 to 500 miles. This would give to the proposed bank all the power it requires. Within such radii it might open a hundred or two hundred branches, and yet hold its entire business within convenient reach. It would be a grave error in such a bank to be ambitious to cover a wider area, and it would be well advised if it only stretched afield from the centre a step at a time, so as to consolidate as it goes. Its most distant branch ought not to be more than 24 hours by rail from the parent establishment, so that in addition to aid, in need, from its neighboring branches, assistance might be readily procurable from the chief office.

The consideration of this question calls to mind what might be termed in one sense, a dangerous if not fatal anomaly in New York banking. As already indicated it is always the commercial centre or metropolis of a country which incubates a panic. From thence the alarm spreads out in every direction, and comes back echo-like, to again alarm timid and returning credit. By these means of recurring, if diminished, fears panics are oftentimes aggravated and always prolonged, causing much injury to the city man, and infinitely more to the distant agriculturist who, like the laborer, has no one but mother earth to pass on his troubles to and who consequently feels the crisis most keenly, although he of all men ought to be furthest removed from the fear of it.

The whole theory of banking is founded on the doctrine of averages. Were it not that the custom of centuries throughout the world has demonstrated that it is absolutely safe to accept the custody of an aggregate of sums of money on the understanding that they are repayable on demand, and yet to spend four-fifths of such sums in the purchase of bills of exchange having many weeks to run it would be hard to convince us that such a course were prudent or even honest banking. Yet under certain well defined conditions it is both. These conditions, however, scarcely contemplate the deposits of assets by banks at far distant points, not readily accessible, and where one prominent feature of banking is its speculative character ; where also call loans are for the most part uncollectable in times of panic, and where there is no Government bank as in Europe to lend safety and solidity to the situation when it becomes alarming.

It is desirable that provincial banks should have their agencies in the metropolis, but it is not necessary that distant banks should leave their money there in bulk. It would be better in every way that the centre of their business should be the nearest city of magnitude, and that the bank which holds their surplus cash should be their own parent institution deeply concerned in and identified with their welfare ; and this the writer says without a shadow of reflection upon the large number of unimpeachable banking establishments and banking houses which are an honor to this great city.

www.ingramcontent.com/pod-product-compliance
Lightning Source LLC
Chambersburg PA
CBHW022035080426
42733CB00007B/837